Spelling Log Book 5–6

By Janey Pursglove
Series developed by Ruth Miskin
Spelling consultant: Jennifer Chew

OXFORD

Contents

Spelling Practice Book 5

Contents (continued)

Spelling Practice Book 6

Using the Spelling Log Book

Why do I need a Spelling Log Book?

Did you know that the English spelling code is one of the hardest to learn in the world? Although we speak all the words in English with only 44 speech sounds, each one of these sounds is often written with many different spellings. For example, we write the ***ay*** sound in lots of ways, including pl**ay**, r**ai**n, m**a**k**e**, **eigh**t and t**a**ble. This means it can be difficult to remember which spelling to use.

The purpose of this Spelling Log Book is to keep a record of the words that you, personally, need to practise more than other words.

How does the Spelling Log Book work?

Sounds charts

If you need a reminder of which sounds are vowels and which are consonants, or different ways to spell the same sound, you can check the charts on pp.6–7.

Speed spell

Every unit, write your corrected words from the Speed spell activity in the space provided on each page.

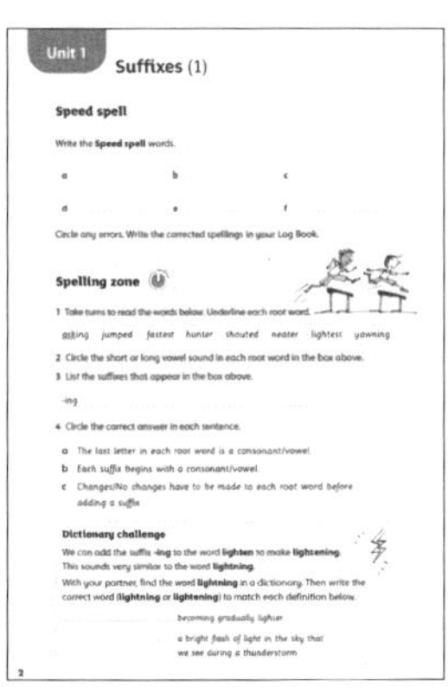

Unit 1 Suffixes (1)

Speed spell

Write the **Speed spell** words.

a b c

d e f

Circle any errors. Write the corrected spellings in your Log Book.

Spelling zone

1 Take turns to read the words below. Underline each root word.

asking jumped fastest hunter shouted neater lightest yawning

2 Circle the short or long vowel sound in each root word in the box above.

3 List the suffixes that appear in the box above.

-ing

4 Circle the correct answer in each sentence.

a The last letter in each root word is a consonant/vowel.

b Each suffix begins with a consonant/vowel.

c Changes/No changes have to be made to each root word before adding a suffix.

Dictionary challenge

We can add the suffix **-ing** to the word **lighten** to make **lightening**. This sounds very similar to the word **lightning**.

With your partner, find the word **lightning** in a dictionary. Then write the correct word (**lightning** or **lightening**) to match each definition below.

becoming gradually lighter

a bright flash of light in the sky that we see during a thunderstorm

2

Words to log and learn

Everyone will have different words that they find hard to spell, so it's important to keep a log of the ones that you personally need to learn. For each unit, use the space provided to write five words in total from Dots and dashes and Word changers that you have found the hardest to remember.

Circle the part of the word you find tricky and explain to your partner why. Take turns to discuss how you will remember how to spell your tricky words.

Words to log and learn

Choose five words from **Dots and dashes** and **Word changers** that you find hard to spell. Write them on p.20 of your Log Book.
Circle the part of the word that you find the hardest to remember.
Explain to your partner why and discuss how you will learn it.

Dictation

Take turns to read aloud one of the dictation sentences from Unit 1, p.62 (Partner 1) and p.63 (Partner 2) for your partner to write down. After each sentence, correct any errors, then swap.

1

2

Four-in-a-row

Choose a word from **Dots and dashes** or **Word changers** and say it to your partner. Ask them to write it down.
Circle any wrong letters. If the word is right, tick a shape in your partner's book. Can you both spell four in a row correctly?

4

Tips

There is a tip on each page to help you remember spelling rules and tricky spellings.

Orange words

When we are reading and spelling Orange words, we have to proceed with caution!

These are common words that even some adults find tricky to spell. We have to work extra hard to learn them. (You might also hear them called Word list words.)

As you meet Orange words in the Jumping orange words challenge, write the ones you need to practise more on p.33.

On pp.34–35 there is a list of all the Orange words you will look at over the year, for your reference. Don't worry – you don't need to learn them all at once! The Orange words you have looked at previously are also listed on pp.36–37 for your reference.

Silent letters

There is a chart on p.32 as a reminder of some common silent letters.

New vocabulary

There is a space to note the meaning of new words that you meet on p.40.

Practice at home

Practise your words to log and learn at home each week. Ask your parent, carer or older brother or sister to call out the words for you to spell aloud or quickly jot down. They should write their initials next to the word each time you spell it correctly. Keep returning to words on previous pages until you are sure you can spell them easily.

Sounds chart – consonants

b as in **b**oot	***c*** as in **c**at	***ch*** as in **ch**ips	***d*** as in **d**og	***f*** as in **f**ish	***g*** as in **g**ate	***h*** as in **h**en	***j*** as in **j**am	***l*** as in **l**eg	***m*** as in **m**oon	***n*** as in **n**et	***ng*** as in ki**ng** ***nk*** as in thi**nk***
b bb	c k ck ch que	ch tch	d dd	f ff ph	g gg gue	h	j g ge dge	l ll le	m mm mb	n nn kn gn	ng nk

p as in **p**en	***qu*** as in **qu**een	***r*** as in **r**ed	***s*** as in **s**un	***sh*** as in **sh**ell	***t*** as in **t**ree	***th*** as in **th**umb	***v*** as in **v**et	***w*** as in **w**eb	***x*** as in e**x**ercise	***y*** as in **y**ak	***z*** as in **z**ebra
p pp	qu	r rr wr	s ss se c ce sc	sh si ti ci ch	t tt	th	v ve	w wh	x	y	z zz s se

* ***nk = ng + k***

Sounds chart – vowels

a as in **a**t	***e*** as in h**e**n	***i*** as in **i**n	***o*** as in **o**n	***u*** as in **u**p	***ay*** as in d**ay**	***ee*** as in s**ee**	***igh*** as in h**igh**	***ow*** as in bl**ow**	***oo*** as in z**oo**
a	e ea	i y	o a	u o ou	ay a-e ai eigh a ei ey aigh	ee e-e ea e y ey ei ie	igh i-e y ie i	ow o-e oa o oe	oo u-e ew ue oe ou

oo as in l**oo**k	***ar*** as in c**ar**	***or*** as in f**or**	***air*** as in f**air**	***ir*** as in wh**ir**l	***ou*** as in sh**ou**t	***oy*** as in b**oy**	***ire*** as in f**ire**	***ear*** as in **ear**	***ure*** as in p**ure**
oo	ar a	or ore oor aw au a ar	air are ear	ir ur er or	ou ow	oy oi	ire	ear eer	ure

Words with silent letter b

Speed spell

Write today's corrected **Speed spell** words here.

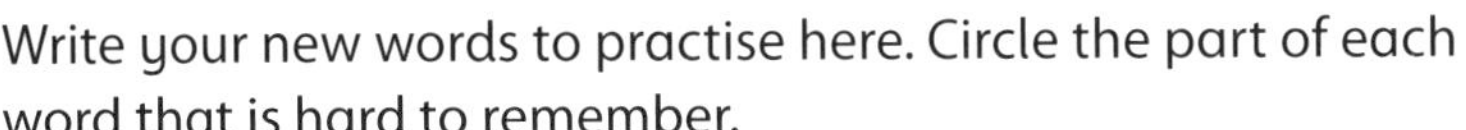

Words to log and learn

Write your new words to practise here. Circle the part of each word that is hard to remember.

Tip: Letters that cannot be heard when we say a word are usually called **silent letters**. Some common words with silent **b** are lam**b**, com**b**, thum**b** and clim**b**.

Words ending in -ible

Speed spell

Write today's corrected **Speed spell** words here.

Words to log and learn

Write your new words to practise here. Circle the part of each word that is hard to remember.

Tip: The **-ible** ending is normally found when the complete root word cannot be heard, e.g. horr**ible** (where you cannot hear horrid). However, there are exceptions, e.g. sens**ible**.

Words ending in -able

Speed spell

Write today's corrected **Speed spell** words here.

Words to log and learn

Write your new words to practise here. Circle the part of each word that is hard to remember.

Tip: When adding **-able** to words ending in **-ce** or **-ge**, we must keep the final **e** to keep the soft **c** and **g** sounds, e.g. noti**ceable**, chan**geable**.

Words with silent letter t

Speed spell

Write today's corrected **Speed spell** words here.

Words to log and learn

Write your new words to practise here. Circle the part of each word that is hard to remember.

Tip: Some words with silent letter **t** have other silent letters in them too, e.g. **w** in **w**restle and **h** in w**h**istle.

Words ending in -ibly and -ably

Speed spell

Write today's corrected **Speed spell** words here.

Words to log and learn

Write your new words to practise here. Circle the part of each word that is hard to remember.

Tip: Words ending in **-ably** are much more common than those ending in **-ibly**. You can usually hear a complete root word before an **-ably** ending, e.g. consider**ably**.

Words ending in -ent

Speed spell

Write today's corrected **Speed spell** words here.

Words to log and learn

Write your new words to practise here. Circle the part of each word that is hard to remember.

Tip: Always use the **-ent** ending after soft **c** or soft **g,** e.g. magnifi**cent**, intelli**gent**.

Words ending in -ence

Speed spell

Write today's corrected **Speed spell** words here.

Words to log and learn

Write your new words to practise here. Circle the part of each word that is hard to remember.

Tip: For some words the noun ends in **-ency** instead of **-ence**, e.g. frequ**ent**/frequ**ency**, dec**ent**/dec**ency**.

The *ee* sound spelt ei

Speed spell

Write today's corrected **Speed spell** words here.

Words to log and learn

Write your new words to practise here. Circle the part of each word that is hard to remember.

Tip: The words **ei**ther and n**ei**ther can be pronounced with the *ee* or the *igh* sound but they are always spelt with **ei**.

Words ending in -ant, -ance and -ancy

Speed spell

Write today's corrected **Speed spell** words here.

Words to log and learn

Write your new words to practise here. Circle the part of each word that is hard to remember.

Tip: A clue for spotting words ending in **-ant**, **-ance** or **-ancy** is if they have a related word with an **-ation** ending, e.g. observ**ant**, observ**ance**, observ**ation**.

Words ending in *shus* spelt -cious

Speed spell

Write today's corrected **Speed spell** words here.

Words to log and learn

Write your new words to practise here. Circle the part of each word that is hard to remember.

Tip: If the root word ends in **-ce**, the ***shus*** ending is usually spelt **-cious**, e.g. vi**ce**, vi**cious**.

Words ending in *shus* spelt -tious

Speed spell

Write today's corrected **Speed spell** words here.

Words to log and learn

Write your new words to practise here. Circle the part of each word that is hard to remember.

Tips: If the root word ends in **-tion**, the *shus* ending is usually spelt **-tious**, e.g. cau**tion**, cau**tious**.
The word **anxious** is very unusual because the *shus* ending is spelt **-xious**.

Words ending in *shul* spelt -cial or -tial

Speed spell

Write today's corrected **Speed spell** words here.

Words to log and learn

Write your new words to practise here. Circle the part of each word that is hard to remember.

Tip: **-cial** usually comes after a vowel and **-tial** usually comes after a consonant.
However, there are some common exceptions. In the words finan**cial**, commer**cial** and provin**cial** the **-cial** ending comes straight after a consonant. In the word ini**tial**, **-tial** comes straight after a vowel.

Suffixes (1)

Speed spell

Write today's corrected **Speed spell** words here.

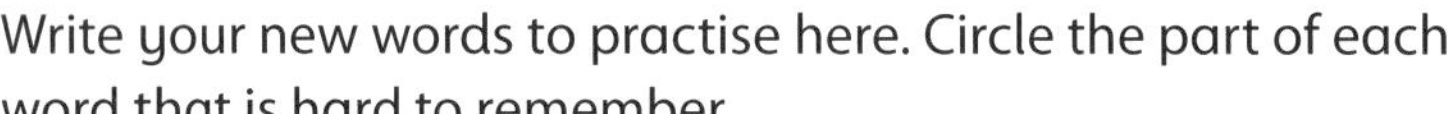

Words to log and learn

Write your new words to practise here. Circle the part of each word that is hard to remember.

Tip: No changes usually have to be made when adding a suffix beginning with a vowel if the root word ends in a consonant.

Suffixes (2)

Speed spell

Write today's corrected **Speed spell** words here.

Words to log and learn

Write your new words to practise here. Circle the part of each word that is hard to remember.

Tip: If the root word ends in an **e**, **drop** the **e** before adding a suffix that begins with a vowel. (The words b**e**ing and s**ee**ing are exceptions.)

Suffixes (3)

Speed spell

Write today's corrected **Speed spell** words here.

Words to log and learn

Write your new words to practise here. Circle the part of each word that is hard to remember.

Tip: Words that sound the same but have different meanings and spellings are called **homophones**, e.g. cereal and serial.

Suffixes (4)

Speed spell

Write today's corrected **Speed spell** words here.

Words to log and learn

Write your new words to practise here. Circle the part of each word that is hard to remember.

Tip: For words ending in **-fer**, we need to think about where the stress comes in the word to decide whether the **r** is **doubled** when we add a suffix beginning with a vowel (e.g. **-ing**, **-ed**, **-al**). The **r** is **doubled** if the **-fer** is still stressed when the suffix is added, e.g. re*fer*ring, pre*fer*red, trans*fer*ring. The **r** is not doubled if the **-fer** is no longer stressed, e.g. *re*ference, refer*ee*.

Suffixes (5)

Speed spell

Write today's corrected **Speed spell** words here.

Words to log and learn

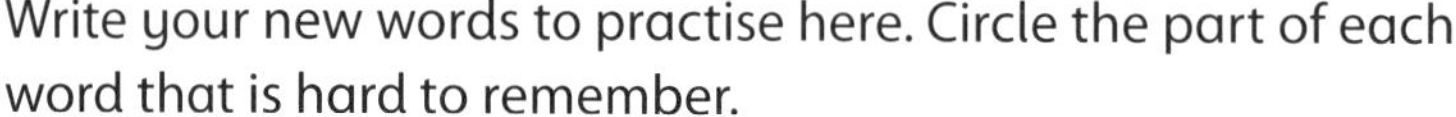

Write your new words to practise here. Circle the part of each word that is hard to remember.

Tip: If the root word ends in a consonant + **y** and has more than one syllable, **swap** the **y** for an **i** before adding the suffix.

happy̸ *happ***i** + **ly** *happ***ily**

The *sh* sound spelt **ti** or **ci**

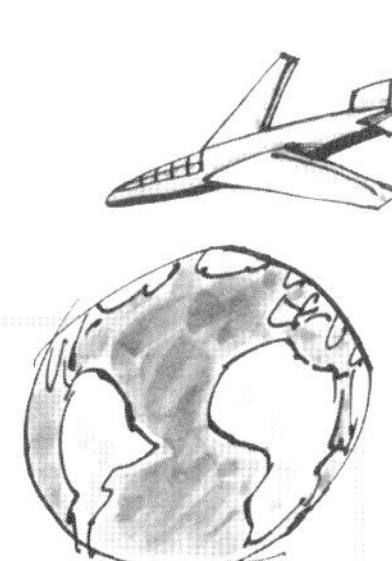

Speed spell

Write today's corrected **Speed spell** words here.

Words to log and learn

Write your new words to practise here. Circle the part of each word that is hard to remember.

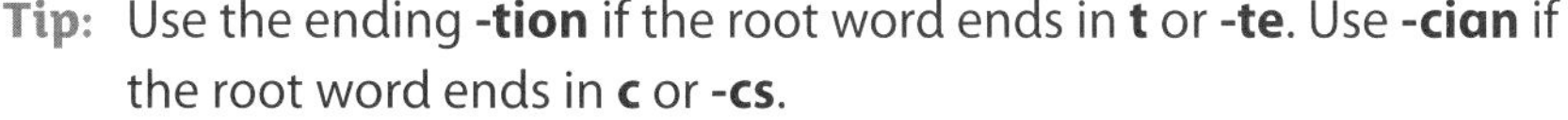

Tip: Use the ending **-tion** if the root word ends in **t** or **-te**. Use **-cian** if the root word ends in **c** or **-cs**.

The *sh* sound spelt si or ssi

Speed spell

Write today's corrected **Speed spell** words here.

Words to log and learn

Write your new words to practise here. Circle the part of each word that is hard to remember.

Tip: Use the ending **-ssion** if the root word ends in **-ss** or **-mit**. Use **-sion** if the root word ends in a **d** or **-se**. (Note that there are exceptions, e.g. attend/attention, intend/intention.)

Silent letters

Speed spell

Write today's corrected **Speed spell** words here.

Words to log and learn

Write your new words to practise here. Circle the part of each word that is hard to remember.

Tip: Try saying the silent letters in words to help you remember to write them, e.g. sound the **k** in **k**nock to remember to include the letter **k**, even though we do not normally hear it.

The spellings ei and ie

Speed spell

Write today's corrected **Speed spell** words here.

Words to log and learn

Write your new words to practise here. Circle the part of each word that is hard to remember.

Tip: The *ee* sound is spelt **ei** if it comes after the letter **c**. It is also spelt this way in prot**ei**n, caff**ei**ne and s**ei**ze.

Words ending in -ible and -able

Speed spell

Write today's corrected **Speed spell** words here.

Words to log and learn

Write your new words to practise here. Circle the part of each word that is hard to remember.

Tip: The **-able** ending is usually used if a complete root word can be heard before it.

Plural nouns (1)

Speed spell

Write today's corrected **Speed spell** words here.

Words to log and learn

Write your new words to practise here. Circle the part of each word that is hard to remember.

Tip: If making a noun plural adds an extra syllable to the word, it is spelt with **-es** at the end.

box *box**es*** *match* *match**es***

Plural nouns (2)

Speed spell

Write today's corrected **Speed spell** words here.

Words to log and learn

Write your new words to practise here. Circle the part of each word that is hard to remember.

Tip: For nouns ending in a consonant + **o** we usually add **-es** to make the plural, e.g. potato/potato**es**. For nouns ending in an **f** or **-fe**, we usually **swap** the **f** or **fe** for **v** before adding **-es**, e.g. loa**f**/loa**ves**.

Silent letters chart

Here is some information about common silent letters.

silent letter	information or spelling tip	example words
k	☆ **k** used to be sounded before the letter **n** in these words	**k**new, **k**nowledge, **k**not, **k**night, **k**nife, **k**nee, **k**neel, **k**nock
g	☆ **g** used to be sounded before the letter **n** at the beginning of these words	**g**nat, **g**naw, **g**narl, **g**nome
t	☆ pronounce the silent letter **t** quietly to yourself when you spell these words	fas**t**en, lis**t**en, sof**t**en, cas**t**le, rus**t**le, bus**t**le, wres**t**le, whis**t**le
b	☆ **b** is silent when it follows **m** or comes before **t** at the end of a word	crum**b**, clim**b**, com**b**, lam**b**, thum**b**, de**b**t, dou**b**t, su**b**tle
u	☆ **u** is silent when it follows **g** and comes before a vowel	g**u**ess, g**u**est, g**u**ide, g**u**ilt, g**u**itar
l	☆ silent letter **l** follows the vowel letters **a** or **o**	sa**l**mon, ca**l**m, ha**l**f, ca**l**f, ta**l**k, yo**l**k, fo**l**k
n	☆ **n** is silent when it follows **m** at the end of a word	hym**n**, autum**n**, solem**n**, colum**n**

Orange words

Write the Orange words that you need to practise.

Orange words chart 5–6

A accommodate ☐ accompany ☐ according ☐
achieve ☐ aggressive ☐ amateur ☐ ancient ☐
apparent ☐ appreciate ☐ attached ☐ available ☐
average ☐ awkward ☐

B bargain ☐ bruise ☐

C category ☐ cemetery ☐ committee ☐ communicate ☐
community ☐ competition ☐ conscience ☐ conscious ☐
controversy ☐ convenience ☐ correspond ☐
criticise ☐ curiosity ☐

D definite ☐ desperate ☐ determined ☐ develop ☐
dictionary ☐ disastrous ☐

E embarrass ☐ environment ☐ equip ☐ equipment ☐
equipped ☐ especially ☐ exaggerate ☐ excellent ☐
existence ☐ explanation ☐

F familiar ☐ foreign ☐ forty ☐ frequently ☐

G government ☐ guarantee ☐

H harass ☐ hindrance ☐

I identity ☐ immediate ☐ immediately ☐

individual ☐ interfere ☐ interrupt ☐

J K L language ☐ leisure ☐ lightning ☐

M marvellous ☐ mischievous ☐ muscle ☐

N necessary ☐ neighbour ☐ nuisance ☐

O occupy ☐ occur ☐ opportunity ☐

P parliament ☐ persuade ☐ physical ☐ prejudice ☐

privilege ☐ profession ☐ programme ☐ pronunciation ☐

Q queue ☐

R recognise ☐ recommend ☐ relevant ☐ restaurant ☐

rhyme ☐ rhythm ☐

S sacrifice ☐ secretary ☐ shoulder ☐ signature ☐

sincere ☐ sincerely ☐ soldier ☐ stomach ☐

sufficient ☐ suggest ☐ symbol ☐ system ☐

T temperature ☐ thorough ☐ twelfth ☐

U V variety ☐ vegetable ☐ vehicle ☐

W X Y Z yacht ☐

Orange words chart 3–4

A accident ☐ accidentally ☐ actual ☐ actually ☐
address ☐ although ☐ answer ☐ appear ☐ arrive ☐

B believe ☐ bicycle ☐ breath ☐ breathe ☐ build ☐
business ☐ busy ☐

C calendar ☐ caught ☐ centre ☐ century ☐ certain ☐
circle ☐ complete ☐ consider ☐ continue ☐

D decide ☐ describe ☐ different ☐ difficult ☐
disappear ☐

E early ☐ earth ☐ eight ☐ eighth ☐ enough ☐
exercise ☐ experience ☐ experiment ☐ extreme ☐

F famous ☐ favourite ☐ February ☐ forwards ☐ fruit ☐

G grammar ☐ group ☐ guard ☐ guide ☐

H heard ☐ heart ☐ height ☐ history ☐

I imagine ☐ important ☐ increase ☐ interest ☐
island ☐

J K knowledge ☐

L learn ☐ length ☐ library ☐

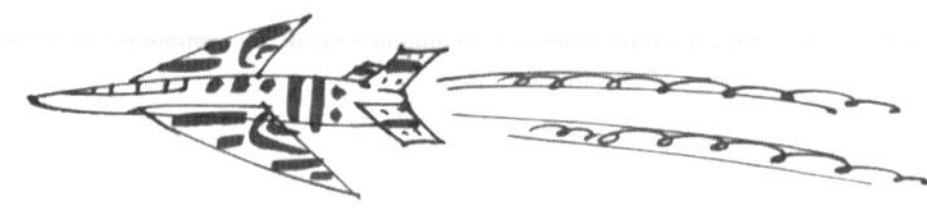

M material ☐ medicine ☐ mention ☐ minute ☐

N natural ☐ naughty ☐ notice ☐

O occasion ☐ occasionally ☐ often ☐

opposite ☐ ordinary ☐

P particular ☐ peculiar ☐ perhaps ☐ popular ☐

position ☐ possess ☐ possession ☐ possible ☐

potatoes ☐ pressure ☐ probably ☐ promise ☐

purpose ☐

Q quarter ☐ question ☐

R recent ☐ regular ☐ reign ☐ remember ☐

S sentence ☐ separate ☐ special ☐ straight ☐

strange ☐ strength ☐ suppose ☐ surprise ☐

T therefore ☐ though ☐ thought ☐ through ☐

U V various ☐

W X Y Z weight ☐ woman ☐ women ☐

Words that are easily confused

Sometimes it is easy to confuse the verb and noun form of a word because they sound the same or very similar when spoken aloud. Here is a reminder of some of the most commonly confused pairs.

advice/advise

- advi**c**e is the noun (*name of a person, object, place or idea*), e.g. He is good at giving **advice**.
- advi**s**e is the verb (*describes what someone is doing*), e.g. I **advise** you to take an umbrella.

practice/practise

- practi**c**e is a noun, e.g. I have tennis **practice** tomorrow.
- practi**s**e is a verb, e.g. I **practise** spelling every day.

licence/license

- licen**c**e is a noun, e.g. My mum has a driving **licence**.
- licen**s**e is a verb, e.g. They can **license** people to drive.

effect/affect

- **e**ffect is usually a noun, e.g. The film had amazing special **effects**.
- **a**ffect is usually a verb, e.g. The drought **affects** us all.

device/devise

- devi**c**e is a noun, e.g. I didn't know how to use the strange **device**.
- devi**s**e is a verb, e.g. I tried to **devise** a new system for sorting the objects to be recycled.

There are some very common homophones and near-homophones that are easy to confuse. Here are some of the most frequently misspelt ones.

it's/its

An apostrophe can be used to show something is missing in a contraction, e.g. I'm = I am, haven't = have not. It can also be used to show possession, e.g. It is Christopher's book.

- **it's** is a shortened version of **it is**.
- When we say something belongs to something, we use **its** *without the apostrophe*, e.g. The elephant swished **its** tail.
- Also watch out for **hers**, *which does not have an apostrophe*, e.g. The book is **hers**.

they're/there/their

These are very commonly confused!

- **they're** is a contraction – it is short for **they are**, e.g. **They're** all going home soon.
- **there** is usually an adverb to show a place, e.g. It's over **there**.
- **their** shows possession, e.g. It's **their** house.

we're/where/were

These sound very similar, but they aren't exactly the same and they mean different things.

- **we're** rhymes with **here** and is a contraction – it is short for **we are**, e.g. **We're** going camping this weekend.
- **where** rhymes with **hair** and is used to talk about a place, e.g. **Where** are you going on holiday?
- **were** rhymes with **her** and is a past tense form of 'be', e.g. We **were** sitting on the beach when the rain started.

bear/bare

- A **bear** is a big, furry animal. The word **bear** can also be a verb that means to carry, bring or take. There is a common expression 'can't **bear** it!' that means to dislike or not be able to cope with something.
- **bare** means uncovered, e.g. Mum said I should cover my **bare** head with a hat, because of the strong sun.

New vocabulary

When you meet a new word and you want to remember what it means, write the word and the definition here.